Listen

HOW EVELYN GLENNIE, A DEAF GIRL, CHANGED PERCUSSION

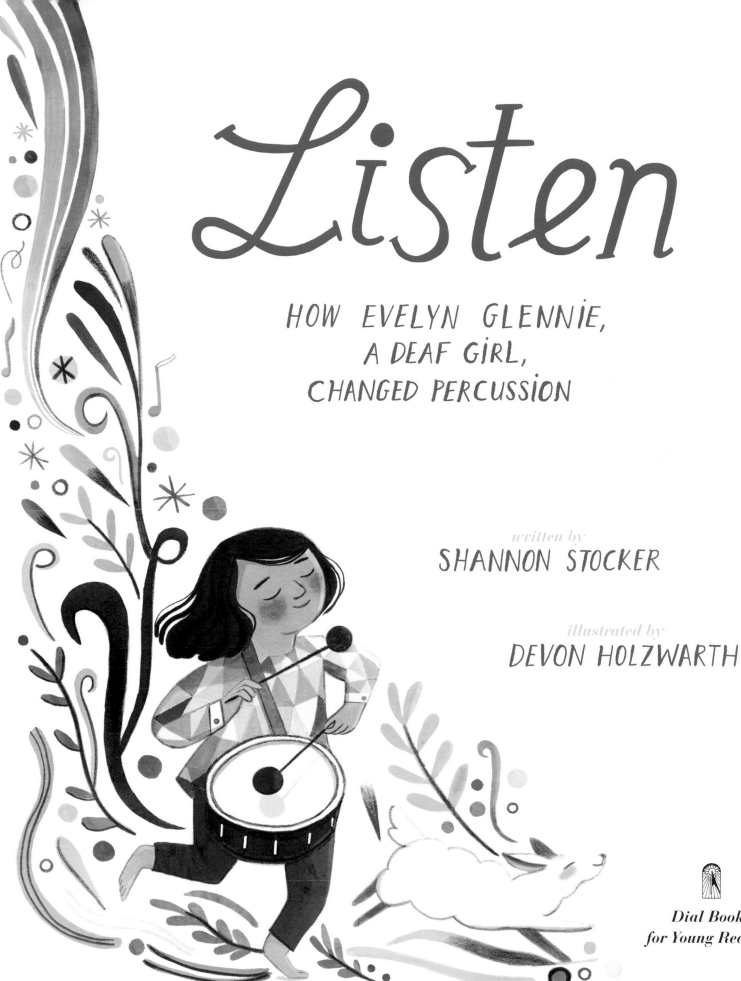

written by
SHANNON STOCKER

illustrated by
DEVON HOLZWARTH

*Dial Books
for Young Readers*

This is a story of music.
Of obstacles.
Of strength and hard work.
Of all you can accomplish when you dream.
If you find your own way to . . . shhhh . . .

listen.

If your ears can't hear the strum,
    or hum,
        or thrum of a melody,
            can music still swirl and whirl?

It did for Evelyn Glennie.

Listen . . .

In the late 1960s, Scottish music rolled through the farm hills of Aberdeenshire, Scotland, where Evelyn Glennie grew up.

Her heart swelled when air blew from the bellows of her father's accordion on Christmas Eve.

On Sundays, she sat on the organ bench next to her mother. A curtain closed behind them, creating their own tiny world of pipes and pedals.

From the moment Evelyn heard her first note, music held her heart.
Evelyn played piano songs by ear at eight years old.

Tink !

Tink !

Tink!

Clarinet notes slid through her lips when she was ten.

But soon, her ears began to hurt.

Voices became distant whispers.

Evelyn's parents took her to the audiologist. He frowned. "The nerves in Evelyn's ears are degenerating. She's never going to be able to play music. She's going to need hearing aids for the rest of her life, and she's going to need to go to a school for the deaf."

Evelyn didn't understand. Only thirty minutes earlier, she'd been able to play music. And now she couldn't? Why? She wanted to wear hearing aids, read lips, *and* play music. She wanted to choose which school she went to.

Evelyn's parents shook their heads at the doctor. "No," her father told him. "Hearing or not, she will do what she wants to do."

After completing primary school at eleven years old, Evelyn decided to
continue her traditional education at Ellon Academy, a secondary school.
By this time, a ringing phone sounded like muffled crunches in her ears.
Still, the percussionists in the orchestra caught her attention . . .

Rat-a-latta
latta-LAT!

danced the snare drum sticks.

DUM-di-da-la
DUM DUM! bounced the marimba mallets.

BUM! WHUM!
BUM!
thrummed the timpani sticks.

Evelyn knew immediately:
I want to be a part of that!

Every first-year student was tested for musical
ability. Questions quietly crackled through a tape
recorder. Evelyn strained to hear.
She scored poorly.

They tested only her
ears' ability to listen.
Not her heart's.
And not her body's.

For the next few months, Evelyn begged the school for percussion lessons. Finally, a percussion teacher named Ron Forbes tested her ability to read music and play rhythms.

Thanks to years of piano lessons, she passed!

For her first lesson, Mr. Forbes gave Evelyn a strange assignment.
He sent her home with a snare drum.
No instructions. No sticks. No stand.
Just a drum.

So Evelyn tapped it.
She pinched it.
She scraped it with her fingernails.
She turned it upside down.

She rubbed her jewelry on it.

Every action created a different vibration.

At her second lesson, Mr. Forbes asked, "How'd you get on?"

"I don't know," she admitted.

He knew she lived on a farm. "How does a tractor feel?" he asked.

Evelyn closed her eyes.

She *felt* the light, tingly squeak of an old, creaky tractor.

She rolled onto the tips of her toes . . .

and she played an old, creaky tractor.

Then, Evelyn *felt* the raucous roar of a brand-new engine. She dug her heels into the floor . . .

and she played the roar of a brand-new engine.

"Evelyn, do you think you could hear more if you took your hearing aids out?"

Evelyn looked at Mr. Forbes as if he had three heads. But she took them out.

Mr. Forbes and Evelyn placed their hands on the wall of the classroom. She watched his lips for direction. "Listen."

He struck the timpani, a big drum that creates big vibrations. *WHUM!*

W H U M !

Then he asked a question that changed her life forever:

"Evelyn, where can you feel that sound in your body?"

He struck the drum again.

Evelyn's whole body resonated—her belly, her back, her legs, her feet! She kicked off her shoes. Her heart raced. *WHUM!* Vibrations moved through her fingertips, her hand, her arm, then crossed her chest and tickled her other arm. Her heart answered, *wha-WHUM! wha-WHUM!*

She had found a sea of sound that belonged only to her! In that moment, every other sense intensified, as if Evelyn's whole body had become one giant ear.

VROOOM

WAH-WAH-WAHHHH

She listened to the buzz
of the wide world around her.

VROOM! Distant trucks zoomed by.

Evelyn's legs listened, hum, hum,
humming with the rattle of the road.

WAH-WAH-WAH. Muffled voices
muttered through an underwater fog.

Evelyn's eyes listened,
turning murmurs into words.

Thrum
hum-hum-hum

Evelyn became so sensitive to
each vibration that she could tune
an instrument based only on where
she felt the vibrations in her body.

When she graduated at the age of sixteen,
Evelyn auditioned for the Royal Academy
of Music in London.

But they turned her down. No one believed a deaf
musician could have a career in music.

But Evelyn believed.

If she could learn to think about listening in a whole new way, then they could too.

Evelyn knew that sound and touch weren't that different. Air vibrated, traveling through the judges' ears before turning into sound. For Evelyn, those vibrations traveled through her body. Her brain just listened differently.

Evelyn fought for the right to audition again. "Does my ability meet the standards of the school?" she asked. They agreed that it did. One board member argued that she deserved a second audition. The board agreed.

Again, Evelyn kicked off her shoes. She looked directly into the judges' wide eyes as she played.

RAT-a
laHa-
laHa
LAT!

Her snare drum sticks danced.

Dum-di-da
la-DUMDUM!

Her marimba mallets bounced.

BUM!

WHUM!

BUM!

Her timpani sticks thrummed.

Everything resonated together—the sticks, the mallets,
the keys, the room . . .

and Evelyn.

This time, they didn't just hear her. They listened.
Her music flowed through their ears and their
bodies and into their hearts.

They welcomed her into the academy. After that, every music school in Great Britain changed its rules. Everyone agreed—no one should be turned away simply because of a disability.

During her second
year at the Royal Academy
of Music, Evelyn entered a
national percussion competition.
She took chances, interpreting the
music her way . . . and she won!

Her heart fluttered when she received
the prestigious Queen's Commendation
for both music and academic excellence.

And, at the age of seventeen, she again kicked off her shoes to perform the very first solo percussion concerto at the Royal Academy of Music.
As she sank into the cushion of broad sounds, the audience sank too.
As she jabbed at short, sharp sounds, the audience jabbed too.

Evelyn played with a freedom that no one had ever heard before.

Europe listened.

Soon, television shows documented Evelyn's life. After graduating, she was invited to perform Bartok's Sonata for Two Pianos and Percussion. The piece was recorded by CBS Records and gave Evelyn the first of two Grammy Awards. She recorded albums and performed in more than forty countries.

And the Queen of England
knighted her, Dame Evelyn.

The world listened.

Evelyn remembered the audiologist who thought people could only hear with their ears.

He was wrong.

"Losing my hearing," she said, "made me a better listener."

Evelyn Glennie became the first full-time
solo percussionist in the world.

She owns nearly three thousand
instruments, all of which sing in her hands.

Throughout her life, many people told
her "No. You can't." But Evelyn always
knew she could.

And you can too.

If you only . . .

shhhhh . . .

listen.

Author's Note

I'm a musician with Reflex Sympathetic Dystrophy. People like me have difficulty with things like temperature changes and pain. When my condition was at its most intense, raindrops felt like knives, and my right arm became much colder than the rest of me. Many parts of my body even forgot how to sweat! Eventually, covered in ulcers and in a wheelchair, I was given two years to live. Like Evelyn Glennie, I heard "You can't" too many times.

But, like Evelyn Glennie, I knew I could.

Perhaps that's why her story captivates me.

I was fortunate enough to talk with Evelyn many times, which allowed me to write a story that reflects her true experiences. During our discussions, I asked her what message she'd like young readers to hear. Her simple answer resonated: "Create your own story," she said. "You cannot wait for things to happen to you. You must make your own opportunities."

It's an authentic message from a woman who has achieved many firsts. She's the first person to ever have made a successful career as a solo percussionist. The first to perform a percussion concerto at London's Royal Academy of Music. The first percussionist to perform a promenade recital at Kensington Town Hall. And many more firsts.

Evelyn hasn't achieved these successes because of her deafness. She's achieved them because of her talent. Hearing or deaf, she was born to play.

"Hearing," she explains, "is basically a specialized form of touch. Sound is simply vibrating air, which the ear picks up and converts to electrical signals, which are then interpreted by the brain. The sense of touch does this too." For Evelyn, this concept dawned naturally when she was a child.

"At that age," she says, "you don't realize you're losing your hearing or going deaf. Your body finds other ways to listen."

She may not listen like a "hearing" person, but she listens nonetheless. And now she's made it her mission to teach the world to listen too.

Soon after graduating from the Royal Academy of Music, Evelyn was featured in her first television documentary, *A Will to Win*, on the BBC. She then recorded and released her first solo album, *Rhythm Song*. As if that weren't enough, that same year (1990), she wrote a book and starred in a second documentary, both entitled *Good Vibrations*.

In 1993, the Queen of England knighted Evelyn by giving her the title OBE (Officer of the British Empire) for her service to music.

She has accepted more than one hundred international awards and honorary doctorates, including two Grammy Awards, the DBE, Percussive Arts Society Hall of Fame inductee, the Polar Music Prize, and Companion of Honour by Queen Elizabeth. And in 2012, she played the beautiful aluminum bells of the Aluphone to lead the Opening Ceremony of the London Olympic Games.

Evelyn has released more than forty CDs, many of them collaborations with other great musicians—Björk, Bèla Fleck, Bobby McFerrin, Fred Frith, Steve Hackett, Mark Knopfler, and more. More than 200 ensembles have welcomed her to their orchestral stage, and 60 of her 120 concertos were written specifically for her.

She's performed in more than forty countries, on five continents. Recognizing the influence these artists have had on her, she aims to inspire others whenever possible through recordings like her TED Talk, "How to Truly Listen," her film, *Touch the Sound*, and a variety of educational YouTube videos.

In addition to performing, Evelyn composes and is a motivational speaker. Though profoundly deaf, Evelyn chooses not to wear hearing aids to this day.

She also continues to perform barefoot, preferring to feel vibrations through the floor.

"My career and my life have been about listening," Evelyn Glennie says, "in the deepest possible sense."

Visit www.evelyn.co.uk to learn more about Evelyn Glennie, one deaf girl who changed percussion.

For Tye, who listens with his heart and never gives up.
I see you. I hear you. I love you.
And for Evelyn, whose bravery shattered glass ceilings
for children everywhere.—S.S.

For Lee Dejasu—D.H.

References

BBC Four. (2014, October 29). *Evelyn Glennie—What Do Artists Do All Day?* (Parts 1 and 2) [Video file].
Retrieved from https://www.youtube.com/user/taran333tula/search?query=glennie

Evelyn Glennie. (n.d.). Retrieved from http://www.drummerworld.com/drummers/Evelyn_Glennie.html

Glennie, E. (2003, February). *How to truly listen* [Video file].
Retrieved from https://www.ted.com/talks/evelyn_glennie_shows_how_to_listen

Glennie, E. (2015, January 1). Hearing Essay. Retrieved from https://www.evelyn.co.uk/hearing-essay/

Henkin, J. (1991, September 13). "Percussionist Plays From Her Heart: Hearing Loss Hasn't Slowed Evelyn Glennie."
Los Angeles Times.

Morrison, N. (2009). "My best teacher"—Evelyn Glennie. Tes.com.

Riedelsheimer, T. (Director). (2006). *Touch the Sound, a Sound Journey with Evelyn Glennie* [DVD]. New Video Group.

Skavlan, F. (2015, November 6). *"Listening is about looking at a person"* —Evelyn Glennie
| *SVT/NRK/Skavlan* [Video file].
Retrieved from https://www.youtube.com/watch?v=VIlfxNHBGE8

Vogel Weiss/PAS, L. (n.d.). Dame Evelyn Glennie.
Retrieved from http://www.pas.org/about/hall-of-fame/dame-evelyn-glennie

Dial Books for Young Readers
An imprint of Penguin Random House LLC, New York

First published in the United States of America by Dial Books for Young Readers,
an imprint of Penguin Random House LLC, 2022

Text copyright © 2022 by Shannon Stocker • Illustrations copyright © 2022 by Devon Holzwarth

Dial & colophon are registered trademarks of Penguin Random House LLC. Visit us online at penguinrandomhouse.com.
Library of Congress Control Number: 2021031440 • Printed in the USA • ISBN 9780593109694

3 5 7 9 10 8 6 4

Design by Jennifer Kelly • Text set in Adobe Garamond Pro

The artwork in this book was rendered in watercolor,
gouache, color pencil, and procreate.

The publisher does not have any control over and does not assume any
responsibility for author or third-party websites or their content.